SPORTS IN THE NEWS
SUPERTEAMS

by Bo Mitchell

T0014181

FOCUS
READERS.

VOYAGER

www.focusreaders.com

Copyright © 2021 by Focus Readers®, Lake Elmo, MN 55042. All rights reserved. No part of this book may be reproduced or utilized in any form or by any means without written permission from the publisher.

Focus Readers is distributed by North Star Editions:
sales@northstareditions.com | 888-417-0195

Produced for Focus Readers by Red Line Editorial.

Photographs ©: Brian Rothmuller/Icon Sportswire/AP Images, cover, 1; Carlos Osorio/AP Images, 4–5; Tony Gutierrez/AP Images, 7; J Pat Carter/AP Images, 8–9; Jeff Chiu/AP Images, 11; Shutterstock Images, 13, 41 (sports equipment); David J. Phillip/AP Images, 14–15; Michael Dwyer/AP Images, 17; Red Line Editorial, 19, 41 (chart); Ringo H. W. Chiu/AP Images, 21; Eric Christian Smith/AP Images, 22–23; Richard W. Rodriguez/AP Images, 25; Rick Bowmer/AP Images, 27; Rich Pedroncelli/AP Images, 28–29; Tony Dejak/AP Images, 31; AP Images, 33; John Swart/AP Images, 35; Reed Hoffmann/AP Images, 36–37; Kathy Willens/AP Images, 39; David Zalubowski/AP Images, 42–43; Brandon Dill/AP Images, 45

Library of Congress Cataloging-in-Publication Data
Names: Mitchell, Bo, author.
Title: Superteams / Bo Mitchell.
Description: Lake Elmo, MN : Focus Readers, [2021] | Series: Sports in the
  news | Includes index. | Audience: Grades 4-6
Identifiers: LCCN 2019054608 (print) | LCCN 2019054609 (ebook) | ISBN
  9781644933947 (hardcover) | ISBN 9781644934708 (paperback) | ISBN
  9781644936221 (pdf) | ISBN 9781644935460 (ebook)
Subjects: LCSH: Basketball teams--Juvenile literature. | National
  Basketball Association--Juvenile literature.
Classification: LCC GV885.1 .M58 2021 (print) | LCC GV885.1 (ebook) | DDC
  796.323--dc23
LC record available at https://lccn.loc.gov/2019054608
LC ebook record available at https://lccn.loc.gov/2019054609

Printed in the United States of America
Mankato, MN
082020

ABOUT THE AUTHOR

Bo Mitchell has lived in Minnesota his entire life and graduated from the University of Minnesota in Minneapolis. Following a lifelong passion for sports, Bo began writing about sports professionally in 1993. He has authored several books and has written about sports for magazines and many websites.

TABLE OF CONTENTS

CHAPTER 1

WHAT IS A SUPERTEAM?

Jordan Bell grabbed the rebound. He dribbled to mid-court as the clock wound down to zero. A smiling Draymond Green raced to meet him and took the ball as a souvenir. The Golden State Warriors had just won the 2018 National Basketball Association (NBA) championship. It was Golden State's third title in four seasons. Players spilled onto the court. The celebration was on.

The Golden State Warriors celebrate after winning the 2018 NBA championship.

Superteams such as the Warriors have been in the news for years. However, a team that wins several championships is not necessarily a superteam. A superteam isn't defined by how many games it wins. Instead, it's defined by how the team is created.

Every sport's history is filled with examples of great teams. It's nothing new when a team drafts a core group of players who improve over time and eventually win a title. But a superteam doesn't happen that way. A superteam comes together quickly when two or more superstars are added to the roster. This can happen when a team trades for a superstar. It can also happen when a superstar **free agent** chooses to join a team.

Superstars are the very best players in the league. At any given time, the league has only a handful of them. These amazing players are in

🔺 Anthony Davis (3) joined the Los Angeles Lakers in 2019 to play alongside LeBron James (23).

the **prime** of their careers. They are old enough to have experience with the game. But they're young enough to play their best. Each superstar could be the top player on almost any team.

Gaining two or more superstars can instantly transform a regular team into a superteam. It happens most often when superstars **conspire** to play together. They agree to join forces even if it means earning less money, sharing the ball more, or leaving a team they've been with for years.

CHAPTER 2

SUPERTEAMS IN THE NBA

Superteams are most common in the NBA. Perhaps the biggest reason for this trend is the nature of basketball itself. Compared to other sports, it's easier for two or three superstars to take over a basketball game. Only five players are on the court at a time. In addition, star players rarely sit out to rest. They also take part in the action on both offense and defense.

LeBron James, Chris Bosh, and Dwyane Wade led the Miami Heat to two titles in the 2010s.

Each NBA team has only 15 players on its roster. And only 13 of those players can be available for a game. Therefore, the best players spend a lot of time on the court. In contrast, each National Hockey League (NHL) team has 20 players. Each Major League Baseball (MLB) team has 26 players. And each National Football League (NFL) team has 53 players.

Thanks to the NBA's smaller rosters, each player has a bigger impact on the game. For example, suppose a team has one superstar and four average players. This team is likely to

➤ THINK ABOUT IT

In hockey, each team has five skaters on the ice at a time. Why do you think it's harder for superstars to dominate a hockey game?

In 2019, Stephen Curry made $42 million from endorsements and $40 million from his salary.

struggle against a team with three superstars and two average players.

Basketball superstars become very famous. In part, they're famous because of small rosters and the opportunity to play most of each game. It also helps that basketball players don't wear helmets, hats, or masks. Fans can easily recognize the best players. And being famous allows them to make extra money by **endorsing** products.

Large, glamorous cities tend to be more attractive to superstars. Large cities typically have more fans and more companies. For example, teams located in New York and Los Angeles often have an easy time bringing in superstars. Meanwhile, smaller cities such as Milwaukee and Salt Lake City have less to offer in terms of glamour. As a result, superstars often join forces on teams in **big markets**.

Some fans may wonder why a team doesn't just sign 15 superstars. After all, the team would be nearly unstoppable. However, the NBA has a **salary cap** to stop that from happening. To keep games as fair as possible, the league sets a limit on how much each team can spend on all of its players. That way, big-market teams that have more money don't end up with all the league's best players.

▲ Miami, Florida (above), is one city that has attracted superstar players because of its size and glamour.

Even so, teams and players figured out a way around that. If two or three superstars join together on one team, the team can still afford to pay everyone. And in many cases, they can also win a lot of games.

CHAPTER 3

THE SUPERTEAM ERA BEGINS

In 1996, Charles Barkley joined the Houston Rockets. When Barkley arrived in Houston, he played alongside Hakeem Olajuwon and Clyde Drexler. Looking back, some fans consider the 1996–97 Rockets one of the first superteams. After all, Barkley, Olajuwon, and Drexler ended up in the Basketball Hall of Fame. However, all three of them were in their mid-30s in 1996. They were no longer in the prime of their careers.

Charles Barkley (4) played for the Houston Rockets from 1996 to 2000.

For this reason, most basketball experts say the Rockets weren't a true superteam.

The 2003–04 Los Angeles Lakers weren't exactly a superteam, either. The Lakers already had superstars Kobe Bryant and Shaquille O'Neal. They added Gary Payton and Karl Malone. All four are now in the Hall of Fame. However, Payton was 35 years old in 2003, and Malone was 40. Both were past their primes.

A true superteam can't be built with players whose best days are behind them. Rather, a superteam is made up of younger players who are at the top of their game. By that definition, it wasn't until 2007 that the superteam **phenomenon** really began. The Boston Celtics brought together Kevin Garnett, Paul Pierce, and Ray Allen. Pierce was 30 and had played his whole career with Boston. The Celtics signed Allen,

▲ Kevin Garnett (5) makes a play during a 2008 game.

who was 32, and traded for Garnett, who was 31. These players transformed a good team into a superteam. Garnett, Pierce, and Allen became known as "The Big Three." They led Boston to a championship that season.

In 2010, LeBron James left the Cleveland Cavaliers and joined the Miami Heat. Most fans agreed that James was the world's best player.

James's friend Dwyane Wade already played for the Heat. Wade was also one of the top players in the game. Adding Chris Bosh gave Miami another excellent player. The Heat went on to win the title in 2012 and 2013. The era of superteams was in full swing.

In 2014, James returned to the Cleveland Cavaliers. He played alongside superstar guard Kyrie Irving. The duo played together for three seasons, and they earned a trip to the Finals each year. After losing to the Golden State Warriors in 2015, the Cavaliers finally brought a title to Cleveland in 2016.

➤ THINK ABOUT IT

Do you think superstars should be allowed to conspire to play together? Why or why not?

Meanwhile, the Warriors had superstars Stephen Curry, Draymond Green, and Klay Thompson. After losing to the Cavaliers in 2016, they signed another one of basketball's best players, Kevin Durant. Golden State defeated Cleveland in the Finals in 2017 and 2018.

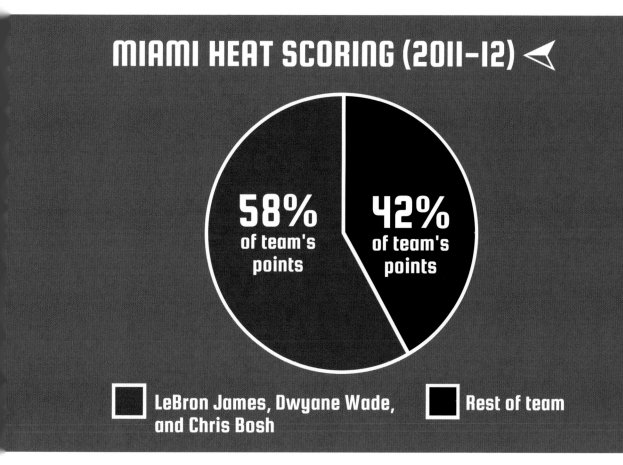

MIAMI HEAT SCORING (2011–12)

58% of team's points

42% of team's points

LeBron James, Dwyane Wade, and Chris Bosh

Rest of team

BUILDING SUPERTEAMS

Owners and general managers are in charge of running teams. They make trades and sign players. However, the trend of players conspiring to play together became a key to building superteams.

In the summer of 2019, Kawhi Leonard and Paul George essentially created a new superteam themselves. Leonard had led the Toronto Raptors to their first championship in 2019. He was named the NBA Finals Most Valuable Player. His contract with Toronto was over after the season, though. So, he became a free agent. That meant he got to choose where he would play next. Leonard was interested in playing alongside another superstar, Paul George.

🔺 Kawhi Leonard throws down a dunk during a 2019 game with the Los Angeles Clippers.

George played for the Oklahoma City Thunder. But Leonard didn't want to play for that team. The two players discussed their options. They had to find a different way to make it work. Before Leonard even became a free agent, George asked the Thunder to trade him to the Los Angeles Clippers. In July 2019, the Clippers made a huge trade to get George, and they signed Leonard. Another superteam was born.

CHAPTER 4

IN SUPPORT OF SUPERTEAMS

Supporters of the superteam phenomenon believe it's good for pro sports. In particular, they point to the benefits it has had for the NBA. More people than ever are watching NBA games. TV ratings continue to grow for both the regular season and the playoffs. More fans are even watching the NBA Summer League. This league gives lesser-known players a chance to develop their skills.

Superstars such as James Harden attract millions of fans to the NBA.

To get fans to tune in, TV networks often show games that feature superteams. Many companies choose to advertise during these games because so many people are watching. NBA teams even started wearing advertisements on their jerseys during the 2018–19 season.

In other words, superteams have been good for business. The popularity of the NBA would likely be growing even without superteams. Still, the excitement surrounding superteams has definitely helped. Due to all the money involved in TV deals, NBA teams are worth more than ever. By 2020, most NBA teams were worth more than $1 billion. Some of the teams in larger cities were worth more than $2 billion.

Fans of superteams enjoy seeing the game played as well as it can be played. And that's what happens when superstars play with one

▲ As of 2019, the New York Knicks were worth $4 billion, making them the NBA's most valuable team.

another rather than against one another. Better yet, with two or more of the league's best players on a team, fans have realistic hopes that they'll be celebrating a championship at the end of the season. That's the best part of being a fan.

The excitement that superteams create also leads to more jerseys being sold. The NBA makes more than $1 billion each season just by selling **merchandise**.

Naturally, many of the game's top players are also in favor of superteams. When superstars conspire to join forces, they do it because they believe they'll have a better chance of winning championships. Basketball players can't play the game forever, so going to a team that gives them a better chance of winning makes sense. After all, the ultimate goal of any player is winning a title. And it's not as if the players or teams are breaking

> ## ➤ THINK ABOUT IT

How would you feel if your favorite basketball team became a superteam? How would you feel if your least favorite team became a superteam?

After nearly a decade with the Oklahoma City Thunder, Kevin Durant won two NBA titles with the Warriors.

any rules by forming superteams. Superstar players figured out a way to give themselves the best chance at winning, so superteams were born.

CHAPTER 5

THE DOWNSIDES OF SUPERTEAMS

Many opponents of superteams believe the phenomenon is bad for sports. Some critics even believe superteams could ruin the NBA. Obviously, the owners of superteams love the popularity and success of their teams. But there simply aren't enough superstars to make every team a superteam. That means most teams aren't superteams. As a result, some teams may go years without reaching the playoffs.

In the 2010s, the Sacramento Kings were a team without superstars. The Kings posted a losing record in every season that decade.

Most professional sports leagues create rules that limit the amount of money teams can spend on players. This prevents rich teams from signing all the best players. But with superteams, the best players have still found a way to play together.

If the league's top players keep forming superteams in the same cities, some fans believe the non-superteams will be hurt. For example, suppose a star player leaves a non-superteam. Without that player, the team will not win as often. As a result, fewer fans will be interested in the team. That will lead to fewer tickets being sold. And fewer people will watch the team on TV. The team will also sell less merchandise. Overall, a team can take a huge financial hit when a superstar leaves.

Most sports leagues attempt to create **parity**. To do so, they make rules that give all teams an

▲ Sales of Cleveland Cavaliers merchandise fell steeply after LeBron James left the team in 2018.

equal chance of doing well. However, some people say the superteam phenomenon ruins parity. It creates a league where only certain teams have a realistic chance to win. If fans feel like their team doesn't have much of a chance, they might stop paying attention. Other fans might start rooting for a superteam instead.

In addition, players who aren't on superteams might feel like they are at a serious disadvantage. Many players may start to believe that winning a title simply isn't possible if they aren't on a superteam.

Some opponents of superteams argue that the phenomenon is risky for the superteams themselves. That's because superteams don't always work. They don't always win a championship. Some don't even make the playoffs. In some cases, players get injured. In other cases, superstars have bad seasons or don't have good chemistry with their new teammates.

> **THINK ABOUT IT**

Can you think of other ways that superteams might be bad for the NBA and other sports leagues?

Despite a lineup filled with stars such as Paul Pierce (34), the 2013–14 Brooklyn Nets failed to meet expectations.

Opponents of superteams say it's not worth it for teams, players, and fans to have sky-high hopes for a superteam that might not work out.

Finally, many fans argue that winning a championship with a superteam can taint the **legacy** of the team. They argue that it's far more impressive when a team has a group of players that develop together over the years. And if that team can take down a superteam, it's even more impressive.

HALL OF FAMERS SPEAK OUT

Many basketball fans believe Michael Jordan was the greatest player of all time. Jordan dislikes the superteam trend. He said the lack of competition is bad for the game. Charles Barkley also opposes the phenomenon. He predicted that superteams will damage the NBA more than help it.

Hall of Famers such as Shaquille O'Neal and George "The Iceman" Gervin said they would rather play for a team that beats a superteam. After all, the game is about competition. And when several superstars are on one team, the game is less competitive. Being on a team that defeats the superteam is more rewarding.

One of the greatest shooters in basketball history, Reggie Miller, agrees. Miller has made it clear that he doesn't like it when great players

⚐ Michael Jordan (23) and Scottie Pippen (33) led the Chicago Bulls to six titles in the 1990s.

leave their teams behind to join other superstars. According to Miller, a superstar player who leaves one team to help create a superteam might get a championship ring. But the player also risks hurting his legacy.

CHAPTER 6

SUPERTEAMS IN OTHER SPORTS

The types of superteams that exist in the NBA are unlikely to happen in North America's other pro sports leagues. But that hasn't stopped teams from trying. The NFL is the most popular league in the United States. The teams have huge sums of money, and the superstar players are very famous. In football, however, each player specializes in either offense or defense. That means nobody is on the field for the entire game.

Even if a football team has an elite quarterback, the team's defense may struggle.

In addition, a football team has 11 players on the field at a time. A basketball team has only five players on the court. Therefore, it's much more difficult for the best football players to take over a game. Not even a superstar quarterback can dominate the way a superstar basketball player can. For example, if the receiver drops the ball, or if the offensive line doesn't block well, a quarterback can't do much to help the team.

Some NFL teams have tried to get enough star players to build superteams anyway. For instance, the Washington Redskins signed several star players in 2000, and the Philadelphia Eagles did it in 2011. The Eagles' quarterback that season, Vince Young, nicknamed them the "Dream Team" before the season even started. He chose the name because the Eagles had so many famous players. But things didn't go according to plan.

The 2011 Philadelphia Eagles finished with a disappointing record of 8–8.

Neither the 2000 Redskins nor the 2011 Eagles even made the playoffs.

Baseball is similar to football in that there are many players on the field at one time. As a result, it is difficult for a few superstars to dominate.

The best starting pitchers can control a game, but they can only pitch every five days. The best hitters might play every day, but they usually bat only four or five times per game.

In MLB, big-market teams such as the New York Yankees, Boston Red Sox, and Los Angeles Dodgers have often had several superstars on their teams. Teams in big cities tend to make more money than teams in smaller cities, so they can afford to spend more on superstar players. Sometimes it works. But often, it doesn't result in more wins.

Hockey is perhaps the closest to basketball, since there are fewer players competing. Each hockey team has six players on the ice at a time. The goalie usually plays the whole game. But the rest of the players take short shifts of less than 60 seconds. They get on and off the ice quickly before getting too tired. Most players spend less than one-third of the game on the ice. In contrast, most basketball superstars play nearly the whole game. For this reason, even the NHL is unlikely to match the NBA's superteam phenomenon.

SUPERSTAR PLAYING TIME ◁

Compared to superstars in other sports, basketball players get far more playing time.

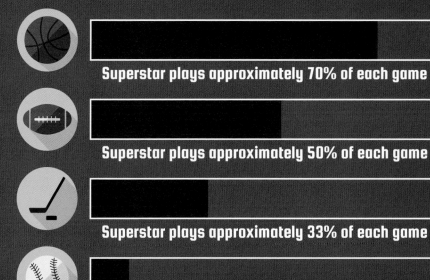

Superstar plays approximately 70% of each game

Superstar plays approximately 50% of each game

Superstar plays approximately 33% of each game

Superstar has approximately 11% of team's at-bats

CHAPTER 7

THE FUTURE OF SUPERTEAMS

Superteams are likely to continue in the NBA as long as they keep bringing in money. If superteams fail to win a lot of titles, the teams and players who build them could face criticism. Or if a huge gap develops between superteams that win all the time and other teams that never seem to win, players and fans might become discouraged. If this situation occurs, it could damage the league and make it less popular.

Philadelphia 76ers superstar Joel Embiid drives toward the hoop during a 2019 game.

On the other hand, if league parity isn't totally destroyed, the debate about superteams could begin to shift. Rather than asking whether superteams are a good idea, people might start asking how best to deal with them. Rules might be changed to enable the small-market teams to be more attractive to superstars. If more teams had a realistic chance of building a superteam, the phenomenon might become more widely accepted.

Whenever a league has financial success doing something, other leagues often try to copy it. Therefore, the success of superteams in the NBA might lead to some form of superteams in other sports. Of course, the games of football, baseball, and hockey are very different from basketball. So, the NFL, MLB, and NHL would need to adapt to make superteams possible.

In 2019, Kyrie Irving (11) joined forces with Kevin Durant on the Brooklyn Nets.

If the superteam phenomenon does expand into other sports, the debates will start all over again. But as long as superteams generate excitement and money, the trend is likely to continue.

FOCUS ON
SUPERTEAMS

Write your answers on a separate piece of paper.

1. Write a paragraph that explains the main ideas of Chapter 3.

2. Do you think superteams are good for the NBA? Why or why not?

3. Which of the following is a characteristic of a superteam?

      A. It must win at least two championships.
      B. It must have at least two superstar players.
      C. It must be located in a small-market city.

4. What would be most likely to happen if basketball teams could spend as much as they wanted on players?

      A. There wouldn't be any superteams.
      B. Big-market teams would sign all the best players.
      C. The price of tickets would go down.

Answer key on page 48.

GLOSSARY

big markets
Large cities with large populations and many businesses.

conspire
To secretly plan something with others.

endorsing
Publicly supporting or speaking in favor of a product, usually in exchange for money.

free agent
A professional athlete who doesn't have a contract with a team and is free to sign with any team.

legacy
How a person or team is remembered.

merchandise
Manufactured goods that are bought and sold.

parity
When a league is balanced so that all teams have a similar chance of winning.

phenomenon
An interesting or remarkable development.

prime
The years when a player is at his or her best, usually the late 20s to early 30s.

salary cap
The upper limit of how much a team is allowed to pay all of its players.

TO LEARN MORE

BOOKS

Braun, Eric. *Basketball Stats and the Stories Behind Them: What Every Fan Needs to Know*. North Mankato, MN: Capstone Press, 2016.

Bryant, Howard. *Legends: The Best Players, Games, and Teams in Basketball*. New York: Philomel Books, 2017.

Murray, Laura K. *LeBron James: NBA Champion*. Minneapolis: Abdo Publishing, 2020.

NOTE TO EDUCATORS

Visit **www.focusreaders.com** to find lesson plans, activities, links, and other resources related to this title.

INDEX

Answer Key: **1.** Answers will vary; **2.** Answers will vary; **3.** B; **4.** B